A CHRISTIAN'S POCKET GUIDE TO

GROWING IN HOLINESS

A CHRISTIAN'S POCKET GUIDE TO

GROWING IN HOLINESS

UNDERSTANDING SANCTIFICATION

J. V. FESKO

CHRISTIAN
FOCUS

Copyright © J. V. Fesko 2012
paperback ISBN 978-1-84550-810-4
epub ISBN 978-1-78191-164-8
mobi ISBN 978-1-78191-169-3

Published in 2012
by
Christian Focus Publications Ltd,
Geanies House, Fearn, Ross-shire,
IV20 1TW, Scotland, Great Britain
www.christianfocus.com

Cover design by Paul Lewis
Printed by Nørhaven, Denmark

CONTENTS

Dedicated

to

Samuel Lee Fesko

whom we never had
the chance to meet
face-to-face.

ACKNOWLEDGEMENTS

Writing a book on sanctification can be a daunting task. Whenever I begin to give thought to my own sanctification in the light of the law of God, I definitely see how far I fall short. But at the same time, I am forever grateful for the gospel of Christ. Were it not for the life-giving verdict in my justification, my sins would eternally stand before me and whisper my unworthiness in my ears. Were it not for my union with Christ and the indwelling power of the Holy Spirit, I would have no power to live for Christ. Paul's powerful words always impart great comfort to my soul, 'I am crucified with Christ, therefore it is no longer I who live, but Christ who lives in me' (Gal. 2:20). So in many ways, to rehearse these truths as I have written this book has given me great food for thought—food for my at times weak and wearied soul. Apart from Christ, I can do nothing.

I want to thank Willie Mackenzie and Christian Focus for approaching me to write this volume. I also want to thank Nic Lazzareschi for his willingness to read over an early draft and offer helpful corrections and suggestions. Thanks are also due to my parents, Lee and Eren Fesko, who read a draft of the manuscript as well. Thanks for your helpful comments! I owe a world of thanks to my wife and children, Val and Rob. Anneke, thank you for your love and constant encouragement. And thank you for your patience and forgiveness when I fail in my sanctification. The same should be said to you, my lads, Val and Rob. I hope you boys grow up with a passion for holiness and that you find the source of your sanctification in your union with Christ—that you would feed upon Christ through Word and sacrament and that you would constantly commune with him in prayer. I also hope that you find a good example in me. I will consider it my greatest failing in life if I do not manifest the holiness of Christ before you, my precious boys.

This book is dedicated to Samuel Lee, our third child. We never got to meet face-to-face. Life is often a crucible where our kind and merciful covenant Lord forms and molds us so that we reflect more and more of the holy image of his son, Jesus—he sanctifies us through life's trials. In this loss, by his grace, our hope lies firmly in the promise that he is a God to us and to our children

(Acts 2:39), and that though Samuel did not come to us,
that we will go to him (2 Sam. 12:23).

⚠ Warning
✎ Don't Forget
⑦ Stop and Think
✴ Point of Interest

INTRODUCTION

When God delivered his people Israel out of bondage from Egypt, he led them into the wilderness, gave them his law, and he told them: 'You shall be holy, for I the Lord your God am holy' (Lev. 19:2). This call to holiness, purity in word, thought, and deed, is still the calling of God's people. But what many do not know is how to be holy. They have placed their faith in Christ but then struggle with how they should obey him. They struggle with sin, at times make progress, but then fall back into the same sinful patterns again. What many people lack is a proper understanding of how to be holy; or in theological terms, they fail to understand what the Scriptures teach about the doctrine of sanctification.

In this small book, the first chapter defines the doctrine of sanctification. I not only explain what it is, but show where the Scriptures teach us about it. In the second chapter, I apply the doctrine of sanctification. So often people do not make the connection between doctrine and practice. The Scriptures know nothing about idle Christians. Rather, as Paul says, sanctified Christians manifest their holiness by 'faith working through love' (Gal. 5:6). In the third chapter, I show how attempts have been made to undermine the doctrine of sanctification. In the fourth and final chapter I offer some suggestions for further reading on the doctrine of sanctification, divided into entry-level, advanced, and classic works.

Throughout the book I make use of a set of documents called the Westminster Standards: the Confession, Larger, and Shorter Catechisms. Our primary authority in doctrine and life is Scripture, but throughout the history of the church, God has gifted some with the ability to teach. In this respect, the Westminster Standards offer an excellent summary of the doctrinal teaching of Scripture.

The Westminster Standards were written by a group of theologians who met at Westminster Abbey in London, England from 1643-52. They were originally tasked with revising the *Thirty-Nine Articles*, the doctrinal standards of the Church of England. But they were soon called upon to write a confession and catechisms that would unite the three kingdoms of England, Scotland, and Ireland in doctrine and worship. The resultant documents were the *Westminster Confession of Faith*, *Larger*, and *Shorter Catechisms*, documents that are still employed by Presbyterian denominations in our own day.

1

SANCTIFICATION DEFINED

What is the doctrine of sanctification? We are not the first people to ask this important question. In the seventeenth century, a group of theologians produced a doctrinal document called the *Westminster Shorter Catechism*. It was intended to be a tool for parents to use in the theological education of their children. *The Shorter Catechism* offers a helpful definition of the doctrine of sanctification: 'Sanctification is the work of God's free grace, whereby we are renewed in the whole man after the image of God, and are enabled more and more to die unto sin, and live unto righteousness' (q. 35).[1] The term sanctification, then, identifies the process of a new believer's gradual transformation from his sin-fallen condition to the perfect, holy and righteous image of Christ.

Though perhaps a bit over simplified, sanctification is the process whereby a person sins less and obeys God's law more. But our sanctification is just one part of our greater redemption. In order to have a better understanding of sanctification, it is helpful to examine sanctification in the broader context of the believer's union with Christ. Once we see how sanctification fits in the big picture, we can then compare the two chief benefits of our union with Christ, justification and sanctification. We will see that our sanctification, or more simply, our capacity for performing good works, is firmly rooted in our union with Christ. We will then explore the two chief elements of sanctification, namely mortification and vivification. Finally, we will examine the relationship between sanctification and redemptive history.

UNION WITH CHRIST

Twentieth-century Reformed theologian, Louis Berkhof, defines union with Christ as the 'intimate, vital, and spiritual union between Christ and his people, in virtue of which he is the source of their life and strength, of their blessedness and salvation.'[2] The doctrine of union with Christ typically appears throughout the Scriptures where we find the biblical expression 'in Christ.' This phrase occurs some twenty-five times in Paul's epistles, though there are other passages that address the subject of union with Christ more broadly. The apostle, for example, likens the marriage relationship to the union that exists between Christ and the church (Eph. 5:25–31); Christ compares his relationship with believers to that of the vine and the branches (John 15:1–17); Peter states that the church is one temple and that Christ is the cornerstone and believers are living stones joined to him (1 Pet. 2:4–5); and Paul likens the believer's union with Christ to that of a soldier's armor (Eph. 6:10–18; cf. Isa. 59:17; 11:4–5; 52:7).

Can you think of any other passages of Scripture that talk about union with Christ?

When we take a closer examination of union with Christ, we find that all of the elements of our redemption are connected to Jesus. We are chosen in Christ before the foundation of the world (Eph. 1:4). We are effectually called in Christ through the preaching of the Word (Eph. 1:13). Those who believe in Jesus and exercise faith have been set apart in Christ (1 Cor. 1:2). Believers are justified, or declared righteous, by faith alone in Christ alone, but this verdict is only given to those who are in Christ (Rom. 8:1). Another benefit of union with Christ is our adoption as sons of God; those who are in Christ are sons of God through faith (Gal. 3:26). When Jesus spoke of his relationship to his people, he did so in terms of the parable of the vine and the branches—those who abide in Christ bear much fruit, or are sanctified. And they persevere to the end (John 15:5–6). Finally, only those who are in Christ are part of the new creation and therefore know that they will be glorified, purged from all sin and imperfection (2 Cor. 5:17).

The entirety of our redemption, commonly expressed through what is called the order of salvation (predestination, effectual calling, faith, justification, adoption, sanctification, perseverance, and glorification) is linked in various ways to our union with Christ. The *Westminster Larger Catechism* helpfully summarizes this point: 'The communion in grace which the members of the invisible church have with Christ, is their partaking of the virtue of his mediation, in their justification, adoption, sanctification, and whatever else, in this life, manifests their union with him' (q. 69).[3] However, even though the entirety of our redemption consists in our union with Christ, this does not mean that the application of salvation is an undifferentiated mass. As John Murray, one-time professor of Systematic Theology at Westminster Theological Seminary, writes: 'When we think of the application of redemption we must not think of it as one simple and indivisible act. It comprises a series of acts and processes.'[4]

In this vein, it is paramount to understand the differences between the legal (or forensic, or declarative) and transformative dimensions of our union with Christ. Or in simpler terms, we must understand and distinguish between justification and sanctification. First,

During the sixteenth-century Reformation the order of salvation was more commonly known as the 'golden chain,' which was based upon Paul's famous verse in Romans 8:30. One of the most famous works that covers the order of salvation is William Perkins' *Golden Chaine*. According to Perkins the golden chain is none other than our union with Christ and this chain is unbreakable.

it is helpful to offer a definition of justification from the *Shorter Catechism*. Justification is 'an act of God's free grace, wherein he pardons all our sins, and accepts us as righteous in his sight, only for the righteousness of Christ imputed to us, and received by faith alone' (q. 33).[5] Now, when we compare justification and sanctification, hopefully the differences between the two become clear:[6]

Justification	Sanctification
Removes the guilt of sin and restores the sinner to all the filial rights involved in his state as a child of God, including an eternal inheritance.	Removes the pollution of sin and renews the sinner ever increasingly in conformity with the image of God.
Takes place outside of the sinner in the tribunal of God, and does not change his inner life, though the sentence is brought home to him subjectively.	Takes place in the inner life of man and gradually affects his whole being.
Takes place once for all. It is not repeated, neither is it a process; it is complete at once and for all time. There is no more or less in justification; man is either fully justified, or he is not justified at all.	A continuous process, which is never completed in this life.
God the Father declares the sinner righteous.	God the Holy Spirit sanctifies him.

A believer's justification by faith alone secures his inde-
fectible standing in the presence of God. In justification,
the legal dimension of our union with Christ, the guilt
and power of sin is broken and Christ's righteousness
(obedience) is imputed to the believer by faith alone
in the legal declaration pronounced by God. As Paul
explains: 'There is therefore now no condemnation for
those who are in Christ Jesus' (Rom. 8:1). Our justification is a one-time act never to be repeated.

By contrast, sanctification is the ongoing process that
removes the pollution of sin and gradually conforms
the sinner to the image of Christ (Eph. 4:20–24). The
sinner's justification definitively sets the believer apart
from the world of sin and God always looks upon him
as holy because of the imputed righteousness of Christ.
The Heidelberg Catechism explains this point as follows:

Q. 60: How are you righteous before God?

A. Only by a true faith in Jesus Christ; that is, though my
conscience accuse me that I have grievously sinned against
all the commandments of God and kept none of them, and
am still inclined to all evil, yet God, without any merit of
mine, of mere grace, grants and imputes to me the perfect
satisfaction, righteousness, and holiness of Christ, as if
I had never had nor committed any sin, and myself had
accomplished all the obedience which Christ has rendered
for me; if only I accept such benefit with a believing heart.[7]

If the believer's standing before God were to hinge
upon his sanctification, his status would always be in

question because of its imperfect nature—we constantly battle against sin (Gal. 5:16–26). Or as the *Westminster Confession* explains it: 'This sanctification is throughout, in the whole man; yet imperfect in this life, there abiding still some remnants of corruption in every part; whence arises a continual and irreconcilable war, the flesh lusting against the Spirit, and the Spirit against the flesh' (13.2). For this reason, as Wilhelmus à Brakel, a seventeenth-century Dutch Reformed theologian, writes: 'In natural order justification comes first, and sanctification follows as proceeding from justification.'[8]

In similar way, John Calvin observed in his *Institutes* that the doctrine of justification is the foundation for sanctification. Calvin writes that justification 'is the main hinge on which religion turns' and that apart from it, we do not have a foundation upon which to establish our salvation nor one on which to build piety toward God.[9] Elsewhere, Calvin explains: 'They,' the impious, 'cannot deny that justification by faith is the beginning, foundation, cause, motive, and substance of the righteousness of works.' Why did Calvin believe this? Calvin explains: 'For unless justification by faith remain unimpaired, the impurity of their works will be detected.'[10] The foundational nature of justification is key, then, not only

The Heidelberg Catechism was written in 1563, in large part, by Zacharias Ursinus (1534–83). Ursinus wrote the catechism for Elector Frederick III (1515–76), who wanted to unite the Palatinate, which lies in what is now modern day Germany, under the Reformed faith. It was eventually adopted by numerous Reformed churches and is still used today by Reformed denominations.

for the preservation of the integrity of our justification, that it is grounded solely upon the work of Christ alone, but also for the integrity of our sanctification. A person cannot bring forward his sanctification, because until his glorification on the last day, it will always be imperfect. Murray succinctly summarizes these points when he writes: 'Sanctification is a process that begins, we might say, in regeneration, finds its basis in justification, and derives its energizing grace from union with Christ which is effected in effectual calling.'[11]

 Though we may distinguish the various elements of the order of salvation, that is, effectual calling, justification, sanctification, etc., we must never separate them. They are inseparable because they all come to us in Christ, and he cannot be rent asunder.

That justification is foundational for sanctification, however, in no way suggests that we can separate the two from one another, that a person can be justified, but not sanctified, or vice versa. This is where the twofold grace of our union with Christ must be maintained. Calvin gives the classic explanation of the twofold grace when he writes: 'By partaking of him,' by which he refers to union with Christ, 'we principally receive a double grace: namely, that being reconciled to God through Christ's blamelessness, we may have in heaven instead of a Judge a gracious Father; and secondly, that sanctified by Christ's spirit we may cultivate blamelessness and purity of life.'[12] In other words, through our union with Christ we receive the inseparable double benefit of the legal and transformative dimensions of our redemption, justification and sanctification. However, once again, Calvin rightly denominates justification as the first blessing and sanctification as the second, as the free pardon of justification provides the indispensable context for the second blessing of our sanctification.[13] As we move forward, we must keep these points in mind as we specifically consider the doctrine of sanctification.

SANCTIFICATION

There are perhaps a number of passages to which a person might turn in consideration of the doctrine of sanctification, but we will begin with John 15:1–17. In this passage Jesus likens himself to the 'true vine' (v. 1), which is in contrast to faithless Israel who was an unfruitful vine (cf. Ps. 80:8–9, 14–15; Ezek. 15:2–4a). There are two types of branches that are joined to Christ, fruitful and unfruitful (v. 2). In v. 3 note that Jesus tells his disciples, 'Already you are clean because of the word that I have spoken to you.' It is this statement that reflects the foundational character of justification (the legal) for sanctification (the transformative). In that, the disciples, except Judas (John 13:11), were 'clean' because of the word that Jesus spoke. The text does not explicitly state it, but the doctrine of justification is in view given how John coordinates the word, belief in the word, and justification. This is evident, for example, when Jesus tells Nicodemus: 'Whoever believes in him is not condemned' (John 3:18); condemnation is an antonym for justification.

Jesus' statement can therefore be glossed as: 'Whoever believes in him is justified.' John also coordinates Christ's word and belief in a number of places: 'And many more believed because of his word' (John 4:41; cf. e.g. 5:46; 7:39; 8:31; 11:40). The disciples, then, are clean because of the cleansing power of the word of Jesus. Jesus is the true vine whom God the Father sends to gather a people and his word wields the redemptive, creative, and cleansing divine power upon those whom he calls. In this respect the word of Christ not only brings about faith by its application through the Spirit, and hence God justifies the sinner, but also creates the context in which the sinner is progressively conformed to the image of Christ.

That it is Christ through the Spirit indwelling, conforming, and sanctifying the justified sinner is apparent in a number of the statements that Christ makes: 'Abide in me, and I in you. As the branch cannot bear fruit by itself, unless it abides in the vine, neither can you, unless you abide in me. I am the vine; you are the branches. Whoever abides in me and I in him, he it is that bears much fruit, for apart from me you can do nothing' (John 15:4–5). The abiding presence of Christ, in a word, union, brings about the believer's sanctification, his growth in conformity to the image of Christ (John 14:15–18). The fruit to which Jesus refers is both the believer's love for and obedience to the Father (John 15:10; cf. 1 John 4:19). Apart from Christ, apart from union with him, a person can do nothing—he is incapable of offering to God either love or obedience.

We can change from the Johannine key and transpose Christ's words into the Pauline key and see the same truths expressed in slightly different terminology. In the eighth chapter of Romans, Paul explains there is no condemnation (or conversely, there is justification) for those who are in Christ (Rom. 8:1). To what end has God justified us? Paul writes: 'In order that the righteous requirement of the law might be fulfilled in us, who walk not according to the flesh but according to the Spirit' (Rom. 8:4). Paul gives the church in Rome the same instruction, though when Christ says, 'Abide in me,' and 'apart from me you can do nothing,' Paul instead says, 'You, however, are not in the flesh but in the Spirit, if in fact the Spirit of God dwells in you. Anyone who does not have the Spirit of Christ does not belong to him…For if you live according to the flesh you will die, but if by the Spirit you put to death the deeds of the body, you will live' (Rom. 8:9, 13). Union with Christ, with the transformative grounded upon the legal dimension, is the source of the believer's growth in holiness and righteousness. As Paul describes the Christian's struggle with sin (Rom. 8:1–17), the forensic declaration (Rom. 8:1) and the subsequent reliance upon Christ through the Spirit (Rom 8:2–4) enables the believer to be further conformed to Christ's image. To this collection of scriptural data we should take note of two important but often-overlooked aspects of sanctification.

First, Christ through the Spirit sanctifies and conforms the believer to his holy image; the believer does not sanctify himself through his own obedience. Take note, for example, that when Paul exhorts the Ephesians to put off the 'old man;' the source of the 'new man,' is God, as the new man is created by him: 'That you put off, concerning your former conduct, the old man which grows corrupt according to the deceitful lusts, and be renewed in the spirit of your mind, and that you put on the new man which was created according to God, in true righteousness and holiness' (Eph. 4:22–4; NKJV). In this vein it is with good reason that Paul calls love, joy, peace, patience, kindness, goodness, gentleness, faithfulness, and self-control the fruits of the Spirit, not those of the believer (Gal. 5:23–4). Paul's famous pithy statement to the church at Galatia best encapsulates this point: 'I have been crucified with Christ. It is no longer I who live, but Christ who lives in me' (Gal. 2:20).

Second, if Christ through the Spirit sanctifies us, then sanctification is by faith alone in Christ alone. We are not sanctified by our obedience but by the work of Christ through the Spirit as we look upon him by faith. Charles Hodge, the famous nineteenth-century Presbyterian minster who taught at Princeton Seminary, explains:

> All that the Scriptures teach concerning the union between the believer and Christ, and of the indwelling of the Holy Spirit, proves the supernatural character of our sanctification. Men do not make themselves holy; their holiness, and their growth in grace, are not due to their own fidelity, or firmness or purpose, or watchfulness and diligence, although all these are required, but to the divine influence by which they are rendered thus faithful, watchful, and diligent, and which produces in them the fruits of righteousness.[14]

Historically, sanctification by faith alone has been expressed in the *Westminster Confession* in the following manner: 'The principal acts of saving faith are accepting, receiving, and resting upon Christ alone for justification, sanctification, and eternal life, by virtue of the covenant of grace' (14.2b).[15] Murray gives an extremely helpful elaboration of the centrality of faith in our sanctification:

> It is imperative that we realize our complete dependence upon the Holy Spirit. We must not forget, of course, that our activity is enlisted to the fullest extent in the process of sanctification. But we must not rely upon our own strength of resolution or purpose. It is when we are weak that we are strong. It is by grace that we are being saved as surely as by grace we have been saved.[16]

Faith alone in Christ alone, then, is as key to justification as it is for sanctification.

Seventeenth-century Puritan theologian, Walter Marshall, summarizes the nature of our sanctification. He focuses on and labors the point of believing rather than doing the gospel—sanctification by faith, not by

Don't Forget: the gospel is not simply for our entry into the Christian life—the program for 'getting in,' and once we're in, we no longer need it. Rather, we need the good news of the gospel every single day of our lives. The grace of the gospel is necessary not only for our justification but also our sanctification.

works.[17] He asks whether we want to be free of fleshly and worldly lusts that war against our souls and hinder us from godliness. The answer to greater growth in holiness is found not in merely believing that gluttony, drunkenness, and immorality are abominations. Christians must move beyond the idea that the pleasures, profits, and honors of this present evil age are vain and empty. Rather, we must believe that we are crucified with Christ. We must believe that we have been raised with Christ and seated with him in the heavenly places. We must believe that we have pleasures, profits, and honors in Christ that are far more glorious than anything we find in the world. We must believe that we are part of Christ's body, the eschatological temple of the Holy Spirit, a citizen of the new Jerusalem, children of the day, not of the night or darkness. We must believe that it is beneath our royal identity and dignity through our union with Christ to practice such sinful deeds.[18]

The only way we can believe more and have greater faith is if Christ grants it to us by his grace through the work of the Holy Spirit. We may struggle with doubt and sin, but in such times we must pray, not only that by God's grace we would repent, but that Christ would cause us to have more faith. With the father of the demon-possessed boy we must cry out to Christ, 'I believe; help my unbelief' (Mark 9:24).

THE PARTS OF SANCTIFICATION

Mortification

There are two constituent parts of sanctification, what theologians have historically called, mortification and vivification. Mortification is the process of putting off the old man, our old sinful existence, dying to the world, and to the sinful desires of the flesh. Paul, for example, writes: 'Knowing this, that our old man was crucified with Him, that the body of sin might be done away with, that we should no longer be slaves of sin' (Rom. 6:6; NKJV). Our old man is our life and existence as we were united to our first federal representative and the deleterious results of his sin, which placed all humanity under the dominion of Satan, sin, and death. In our mortification, we therefore put to death our sinful desires, ways, and conduct. As John Owen, the well-known seventeenth-century Reformed theologian, writes: 'To kill a man, or any other living thing, is to take away the principle of all his strength, vigour, and power, so that he cannot act or exert, or put forth any proper actings of his own.'[19] The legal claims Satan, sin, and death held over believers is eliminated in our justification but the abiding remnants still remain in a person. Therefore, mortification is a life-long process and is not complete until a believer's glorification—until the believer dies and has every vestige of sin removed from him.

In the meantime, the time between our conversion and our glorification, we must be diligent to guard against unchecked sinful habits and conduct. Owen identifies six different symptoms that possibly indicate an inattention to sin: (1) a habit of unchecked sin; (2) denial that there is a problem with sin despite strong evidence to the contrary; (3) frequently choosing sinful instead of godly conduct; (4) resisting sin only because of the consequences; (5) delaying action against sin knowing that as long as God does not discipline, there is freedom to sin; and (6) ignoring sin because you have already withstood discipline from God.[20] Owen astutely comments that for the person in whom these signs are found, 'Unspeakable are the evils which attend such a frame of heart.'[21]

Regardless of the state of a person's sanctification, whether weak or strong, the key to putting the old man to death is to look by faith to Christ. More will be said about this in the following chapter, sanctification applied. But a person must use the means that Christ has placed at his disposal—Word, sacrament, and prayer. Just as a person cannot survive unless he eats a healthy diet, a person must feed upon Christ through the reading of the Word, attending to the preaching of the Word, a regular use of the sacrament of the Lord's Supper, and diligent prayer. Moreover, a person must recognize that no amount of human effort will subdue the old man. Rather, the old man has been subjected to the power of the Holy Spirit, and it is the Spirit who continues to mortify the old man. The Holy Spirit makes the reading, preaching and administration of the Lord's Supper an effectual means of mortification. Through these means of grace, following Paul's instruction, a person can 'seek the things that are above, where Christ is, seated at the right hand of God.' We can set our 'minds on things that are above, not on things that are on earth' (Col. 3:1–2). Owen expresses Paul's point in this manner: 'Set faith at work on Christ for the killing of thy sin. His blood is the great sovereign remedy for sin-sick souls. Live in this, and thou wilt die a conqueror. Yea, thou wilt through the good providence of God, live to see thy lust dead at thy feet.'[22]

Vivification

The second part of sanctification is vivification, which is the process of putting on the new man. That is, seeking life through our new federal representative, Jesus. Paul writes: 'Do not lie to one another, since you have put off the old man with his deeds, and have put on the new man who is renewed in knowledge according to the image of Him who created him' (Col. 3:9–10; NKJV). A Christian does not merely refrain from sin but rather engages in holy, righteous, and godly conduct, whether in word, thought, or deed. Note, for example, how Paul contrasts the Christian's existence as the old and new man:

> If indeed you have heard Him [Christ] and have been taught by Him, as the truth is in Jesus: that you put off, concerning your former conduct, the old man which grows corrupt according to the deceitful lusts, and be renewed in the spirit

of your mind, and that you put on the new man which was created according to God, in true righteousness and holiness. (Eph. 4:21–4; NKJV)

By putting off of the old man (mortification) the Christian seeks to put on the new man (vivification).

Paul then goes on to explain the Christian's transformation in terms of his ethical conduct: 'Therefore, having put away falsehood, let each one of you speak the truth with his neighbor, for we are members one of another' (Eph. 4:25). The Christian does not merely refrain from deceit but also speaks the truth. Paul writes:

Let the thief no longer steal, but rather let him labor, doing honest work with his own hands, so that he may have something to share with anyone in need. Let no corrupting talk come out of your mouths, but only such as is good for building up, as fits the occasion, that it may give grace to those who hear. (Eph. 4:28–9)

In his mortification, the Christian refrains from theft and also freely gives of his possessions to others; the slanderer no longer speaks evil of his friends but instead utters words of kindness, love, and encouragement. In our sanctification, we are not simply cleansed of sin but also enabled to perform righteousness.

What are the two parts of our sanctification? How might you pray to grow in these areas in your Christian walk?

SANCTIFICATION IN REDEMPTIVE HISTORY

As important as sanctification is to the individual Christian, it is crucial to connect sanctification to the broader scope of redemptive history. In other words, when God set out to redeem a people for himself, he did so as part of a larger plan to redeem the entire creation. The first heavens and earth were created and placed under the dominion of Adam and Eve. The psalmist recounts the glorious and honored place that the son of man had over the sheep, oxen, beasts of the field, the birds of the heavens, and fish of the sea—all of these creatures were placed 'under his feet' (Ps. 8). But Adam rebelled and forfeited his exalted place as God's vicegerent. The prophet Daniel had a vision where he saw the beasts exercising dominion over the creation—a reversal of the created order—the consequences of Adam's sin (Dan. 7:1–11). But Daniel's vision did not end with the beasts permanently exercising dominion. Rather, the Ancient of Days appeared and 'their dominion was taken away' (Dan. 7:12). Who was to fill the power vacuum? Daniel saw 'one like the son of man,' one like Adam, coming on the clouds: 'And to him was given dominion and glory and a kingdom, that all peoples, nations, and languages should serve him; his dominion is an everlasting dominion, which shall

Did you know that the Bible is its own interpreter? The Bible frequently explains other portions of Scripture. In the large scale, the New Testament interprets the Old Testament, and earlier portions of the Old Testament are interpreted by later portions.

not pass away, and his kingdom one that shall not be destroyed' (Dan. 7:14). Who is this one like the son of man, like Adam? Jesus Christ.

When the religious leaders interrogated Jesus he was asked whether he was the Messiah, the Son of God. To answer the question Jesus invoked the imagery from Daniel: 'You have said so. But I tell you, from now on you will see the Son of Man seated at the right hand of Power and coming on the clouds of heaven' (Matt. 26:64). Because of his obedience to the law, fulfilling every jot and tittle (Matt. 5:17); because of his suffering and death on the cross, fulfilling the requirement for the penalty of the law; and his resurrection from the dead, the indication that his sacrifice was accepted by the Father; Christ was given all authority in heaven and on earth (Matt. 28:18–20). Or as Paul writes:

> He made himself nothing, taking the form of a servant, being born in the likeness of sinful men. And being found in human form, he humbled himself by becoming obedient to the point of death, even death on a cross. Therefore God has highly exalted him and bestowed on him the name that is above every name, so that at the name of Jesus every knee should bow, in heaven and on earth and under the earth, and every tongue confess that Jesus Christ is Lord, to the glory of the Father. (Phil. 2:7–11)

In another place, Paul quotes the language of Psalm 8 and applies it to Jesus. Paul says that Jesus must reign, 'until he puts all his enemies under his feet' (1 Cor. 15:25). He goes on, 'For "God has put all things in subjection under his feet"' (1 Cor. 15:27).

The similarities between Adam and Jesus are no coincidence, as Paul calls Adam a 'type of the one who was to come' (Rom. 5:14). That is, Adam foreshadowed the person and work of Christ. Paul further elaborates upon the connections between Adam and Christ when he writes: 'The Scriptures tell us, 'The first man, Adam, became a living person.' But the last Adam—that is, Christ—is a life-giving Spirit' (1 Cor. 15:45; NLT). The two Adams are the head of two different creations, the fallen creation and the new heavens and earth written about in the prophet Isaiah (Isa. 65–6, esp. 65:17; 66:22) and the book of Revelation (Rev. 21:1ff). Jesus pours out the Holy Spirit upon the creation unleashing the creative and renewing power of the triune God. Just as the Son of God brought the first creation into existence through the spoken word and the power of the Spirit, so too through the all-powerful gospel applied by the Spirit people are raised from death to life and the new heavens and earth are unleashed (Col. 1:16; John 1:3; Gen. 1:1–3). The epicenter of the new creation is found in the church of Jesus Christ: 'Therefore, if anyone is in Christ, the new creation has come: The old has gone, the new is here' (2 Cor. 5:17; TNIV)! All of this biblical data should always be coordinated with the individual's personal sanctification.

When a person is united to Christ by faith, he is indwelled by the Holy Spirit, the power of the age to come (Heb. 6:5). The believer's transformation, the death of the old man, and continued increased conformity to the image of Christ, is but one small part of the advent of the new heavens and earth. The old fallen creation is marked by 'sexual immorality, impurity, sensuality, idolatry, sorcery, enmity, strife, jealousy, fits of anger, rivalries, dissensions, divisions, envy, drunkenness, orgies, and things like these' (Gal. 5:19–21). In complete contrast, Christ unfurls the new creation in the midst of the sin-darkened, fallen, old creation. In the midst of the darkness, Christ through the Spirit shines forth the light of 'love, joy, peace, patience, kindness, goodness, faithfulness, gentleness,' and 'self-control' (Gal. 5:22–3). Therefore, the believer's progressive transformation is part of this greater historical tapestry that will be completed on the last day, when the last trumpet sounds, Christ returns, the dead in Christ arise, those who are still alive join Christ in the air with those who have been raised, and we are all transformed in the twinkling of an eye (1 Cor. 15:52; 1 Thess. 4:17).

CONCLUSION

The only way we can become holier and manifest truly good works is through our union with Christ. When we are united to Christ by faith, and we have our legal status permanently secured in our justification, then, and only then, can we know that we have a foundation upon which we can build a life of piety. In our justification we no longer have God as our judge but as our Father. Christ our brother has laid down his life for us and poured the

Holy Spirit upon us so that he might indwell us. Paul's words should echo in our hearts—we have been crucified with him, therefore we no longer live, but Christ now lives in us. Only when we abide in him will we produce fruit; only when we abide in him will we grow in our sanctification and conformity to Christ's image.

In our living the Christian life, we must always rely upon Christ to transform and change us. On our own, we are incapable of changing ourselves. But what is impossible for humans is possible with God.

2

SANCTIFICATION APPLIED

In the previous chapter we explored and defined the doctrine of sanctification biblically and theologically. But biblical doctrine was never intended for mere or idle contemplation. True doctrine always has two goals, practice and worship. When God saves a person from his sin-fallen estate it is so that once he is saved, he will live a life of holiness and righteousness. However, when a person manifests the righteousness of Christ, the purpose is not self-aggrandizement. Rather, the saved person should ultimately be filled with praise and thanksgiving for the one who saved him. He will not sing of his own accomplishment, 'I did it!' Rather he will sing of Christ's work, 'He did it for me!' If you were drowning in a turbulent ocean and a lifeguard risked her life to save you, common sense dictates that you would enthusiastically thank her. The parallel between being pulled from the ocean and being saved from sin and death is not precise but nevertheless close enough to make the point. God is worthy of praise and worship simply for who he is apart from any consideration for what he has done. But when we consider what he has done in Christ through the Spirit in the salvation of sinful people, we should especially be moved to praise and thanksgiving. In terms of older theology, the *Heidelberg Catechism* is divided into three main sections, which have been labeled: guilt, grace, and gratitude. In other words, Christians live in gratitude, not out of a sense of repaying a debt, but thanksgiving.

But the question remains, what does the doctrine of sanctification look like in practice? How is it applied? I propose to address these questions in the following manner. First, we must understand the means of our sanctification, namely our transformation through Word, sacrament, and prayer. Second, we have to recognize the churchly context of our sanctification—we are saved to be part of the body of Christ, the church, and for this reason the church is the center of gravity for sanctification in practice. Therefore we will explore the connections

The work of our redemption, from beginning to end, is a work of the triune God, Father, Son, and Holy Spirit.

between sanctification and the church. Third, and last, we will examine a few concrete illustrations of sanctification in action.

THE MEANS OF OUR SANCTIFICATION

The Word of God is powerful, to say the least. All we have to do is open the first page of the Bible and we can read of its power and might. There was a time when there was no time—it did not exist. And there was a point when there was nothing but the triune God. There was God and there was nothing. But God spoke and out of nothing (*ex nihilo*) the creation came into existence. Time began with the creation of space and as the voice of God pierced the darkness, worlds came into existence. As the author of Hebrews writes: 'By faith we understand that the universe was created by the Word of God, so that what is seen was not made out of things that are visible' (Heb. 11:3). God could have chosen to create in a number of different ways but ultimately decided to do so through the spoken word. Unlike human beings, who can utter thousands upon thousands of words to no effect, when God speaks, things happen. The connection between the Word of God and creation is not an isolated case of an exhibition of God's power. Rather, the same means by which God brought worlds into existence is the same means by which he saves people from sin and death.

The apostle Paul famously opens his letter to the Romans with the following words: 'For I am not ashamed of the gospel, for it is the power of God for salvation to everyone who believes, to the Jew first and also to the Greek' (Rom. 1:16). The message of the gospel is the Word of God applied to sinful human beings. Later in Romans, Paul explains the means by which God brings the gospel to bear upon sinners. Paul writes: 'For with the heart one believes and is justified, and with the mouth one confesses and is saved...How then will they call on him in whom they have not believed And how are they to believe in him of whom they have never heard?' Paul supplies the answer in his rhetorical question: 'And how are they to hear without someone preaching' (Rom. 10:10-14). God brings his all-powerful creative word to bear upon sinners through the preaching of the gospel. As Paul writes: 'So faith comes from hearing, and hearing through the word of Christ' (Rom. 10:17). What we may not realize is that Paul's words reveal the manner in which a person's transformation occurs.

There is an old cliché, 'You are what you eat.' A similar dictum exists in the computing world. GIGO is the acronym for the computer-programming maxim, 'Garbage in, garbage out.' The truth captured in these statements is not limited to the worlds of eating and computing, but also applies to the disparate ends of salvation and damnation. The Scriptures acknowledge that idols have no existence—they are blocks of wood or stone that people fashion with their own hands. The psalmist says of these blocks of silver and gold (Ps. 115:5-7):

They have mouths, but do not speak;
eyes, but do not see.
They have ears, but do not hear;
noses, but do not smell.
They have hands, but do not feel;
feet, but do not walk;
and they do not make a sound in their throat.

What happens to people who make these idols? The psalmist baldly states: 'Those who make them become like them; so do all who trust in them' (Ps. 115:8). This type of deformation is precisely what happened to Israel during the prophet Isaiah's ministry. Rather than worshipping the one true God, they instead turned to idols. God therefore turned them over to their sin and they became ever looking, but never seeing, ever listening, but never hearing—they became dull and never understood God's prophetic word. In the case of Old Testament Israel's idolatry, they became what they worshipped.[23]

The exact opposite is true for those who worship the one true living God. Just as Moses' face was illuminated and transformed for a time just from being in the presence of God, so there is a greater transformation for the people

If the gospel and preached word is the power of God unto salvation, how consistently do you expose yourself to the word? How regularly do you read your Bible and attend worship to hear the preaching of the word?

who draw near to God through Christ in the Spirit. God speaks his words of salvation through the preaching of the gospel and sends forth his Spirit into the church. The dead are raised to life, as a person who was once dead in her sins and trespasses is brought to life by the Spirit's application of the Word of God. But the transformative and life-changing power of the gospel is not reserved merely for our entry-point into the Christian life, merely for our conversion. Rather, the gospel is the power of God unto salvation, even our sanctification, throughout the entirety of our earthly pilgrimage, the entirety of our lives. As God unleashes his word into the midst of his people through preaching, people's lives are changed. The people of God mortify their old man and vivify their new man. In a word, we become like the one we worship.

THE CHURCHLY CONTEXT OF SANCTIFICATION

We have identified the means by which God not only converts but also sanctifies sinners, through the preaching of the Word of God. But the question remains, where can we find the Word of God? The answer is simple, we find the Word in the church. It is true, people can find the Word of God in their own homes as many, if not most, Christians own a copy of the Bible. They can read the Bible any time they choose and often do so as part of a regular regimen of daily devotions. Personal devotional time is certainly an important part of a healthy spiritual life. However, personal devotion time is not the main staple of a person's spiritual diet. Rather, attending to the preaching of the Word and the administration of the sacraments is the main staple of a person's spiritual diet.

When God gave his word to his people, he did not do so indiscriminately. In the Old Testament, God specifically gifted and inspired prophets to preach his Word to his people. But now, since the advent of Christ, God has spoken to us through his Son and through Christ's outpouring of the Holy Spirit upon the church, Jesus has gifted certain men to preach his Word. The fruits of the Spirit (love, joy, peace, patience, kindness, goodness, gentleness, and self-control) are supposed to be manifested by all Christians. The fruit of the Spirit has been democratized among the people of God. The gifts of the Spirit, on the other hand, are sovereignly dispensed at the discretion of the triune Lord. Paul writes, for example: 'God arranged the members in the body, each one of them, as he chose….And God has appointed in the church first apostles, second prophets, third teachers, then miracles, then gifts of healing, helping, administrating, and various kinds of tongues' (1 Cor. 12:18, 28). Paul's list of spiritual gifts is instructive and immediately informs us that not all of these gifts are universally dispensed. After all, not just anyone has the opportunity to be an apostle, for example. What, however, about pastors? Paul does not mention pastors in this list of gifts.

Paul's list of spiritual gifts in 1 Corinthians is not exhaustive, as his list from Ephesians makes clear. In Ephesians Paul identifies other gifts of the Spirit: 'And he gave some, apostles; and some, prophets; and some, evangelists; and some, pastors and teachers; For the perfecting of the saints, for the work of the ministry, for the edifying of the body of Christ' (Eph. 4:11–12; KJV). Paul identifies pastors as a gift of Christ to the church that comes through the outpouring of the Spirit. Paul then states that pastors, those who preach the Word of God, are those specific individuals that God has chosen to herald the life-changing power of the Word of God. These pastors do not wield the Word for their own personal gain or fortune but, as Paul clearly states, for the 'perfecting of the saints.' In other words, preachers herald the Word to edify, or build-up, the body of Christ. Preachers herald the gospel, the Word of God, not simply for the salvation of God's people but also for their sanctification. Though Paul was an apostle, he was also a pastor, as the Spirit can dispense multiple gifts to one individual. In Paul's case, notice the purpose behind Paul's preaching: 'This letter is from Paul, a slave of God and an apostle of Jesus Christ. I have been sent to proclaim faith to those God has chosen and to teach them to know the truth that shows them how to live godly lives' (Titus 1:1; NLT).

But preachers herald the Word of God in two primary forms—the spoken and sacramental word. When a pastor preaches, he proclaims the audible Word of God—the Word goes out and strikes listeners in their ears. Through the work of the Spirit they hear the Word and the Spirit applies it to their lives. In the case of the visible words, or baptism and the Lord's Supper, what the word is to the ears the sacraments are to the other senses. The sacraments visibly and tactilely preach the Word to our senses—we feel the water upon us, we taste, feel, and smell the bread and wine. The sacraments do not ever function independently of the Word; one can have the preaching of the Word alone but never the sacraments alone. The sacraments require the Word—they seal and confirm it. When a minister preaches about the crucified Christ, he then takes the bread and wine and reminds the church that it is sacramentally the body and blood of Christ—his body broken and his blood shed for them. The Holy Spirit employs the audible and visible Word of God to bring about the greater sanctification of God's people. This is not a novel conclusion but has been acknowledged and practiced by the church. *The Westminster Larger Catechism* asks: 'How is the Word made effectual to salvation?' The catechism answers:

> The Spirit of God makes the reading, but especially the preaching of the Word, an effectual means of enlightening, convincing, and humbling sinners; of driving them out of themselves, and drawing them unto Christ; of conforming them to his image, and subduing them to his will; of strengthening them against temptations and corruptions; of building them up in grace, and establishing their hearts in holiness and comfort through faith unto salvation. (q. 155)[24]

Given the function of the Word in our sanctification, the Westminster divines therefore call the sacraments 'effectual means of salvation' (q. 161). There is no magical quality to Word and sacrament. The Bible is not a book of incantations to be invoked to bring about magical results. Likewise, the sacraments are not mysterious substances to be consumed that magically impart eternal life. Rather, they are the chosen means by which the triune God communicates his life-giving Word and applies them through faith alone in the hearts and lives of the recipients who receive them.

We must not think that the sacraments have any magical power to them so that all we must do is sprinkle the water or eat the bread and drink the wine. The sacraments are not magic tricks but rather God's authoritative seal upon the preached Word. The sacraments are empty signs without the preaching of the Word of God.

SANCTIFICATION IN ACTION

So, then, what does sanctification look like in practice? The picture that the Scriptures portray is very simple and unencumbered. Each and every Lord's day a person who is united to Christ should go to church and attend to the preaching of the Word and the administration of the sacraments. True, a person should be baptized only once, but when others are baptized those sitting in the pew should never be idle observers but participants in the sacred rite. They see the gospel proclaimed in the administration of the sacrament. As they hear the Word and see it by faith, the Spirit makes the Word an effectual means of a person's sanctification. *The Westminster Larger Catechism* has wonderful counsel for how a person is supposed to attend to the preaching of the Word:

> It is required of those that hear the Word preached, that they attend upon it with diligence, preparation, and prayer; examine what they hear by the Scriptures; receive the truth with faith, love, meekness, and readiness of mind, as the Word of God; meditate, and confer of it; hide it in their hearts, and bring forth the fruit of it in their lives. (q. 160)

In attending to the preaching of the Word, a person must pay close attention, pray that she will hear the message, compare it against the Scriptures, meditate upon it, seek to memorize the passage that was preached, and then put into practice what was preached. If we recognize that God speaks to his people through the preaching of the Word, then perhaps we will give more attention to it than we would a speech at the local Rotary Club.

In addition to attending to the preaching of the Word each Lord's Day, a healthy spiritual diet involves supplements, such as the daily devotional reading of the Scriptures. All too often people hardly touch their Bibles let alone read them. As a pastor, commanded to know the condition of my flock, I made a point of not bringing my Bible when I performed pastoral visits. When conversation eventually came around to questions about the Bible, I would ask the person I was visiting if I could borrow their copy. My intention was to see how quickly or slowly a person could find his Bible. If it was Thursday and a person told me that he forgot his Bible in the car on Sunday, then chances were that he had not read his Bible for nearly four days. An inattention to the Scriptures is often the symptom of greater spiritual problems. If we find time to eat, bathe, and perform daily hygiene, perhaps such habits can inform our daily intake of Scripture. While you eat your breakfast in the morning, spend some time feeding your soul by reading your Bible. Attending to the preaching of the Word, the sacraments, and the daily reading of Scripture are indispensible parts of improving our sanctification.

Another crucial element of a healthy spiritual diet is regular attention to prayer. Prayer is often one of the neglected elements in a person's spiritual walk. Prayer is the means by which we offer up our desires unto God and is the arena in which we often wrestle with him in the struggle to seek greater sanctification. In prayer we can cry aloud to God and ask him to sanctify us further. Do you lack faith? Plead with God that he would strengthen it. Do you lack hope? Pray to God that he would fill you with it. In prayer, we look to the risen and ascended Messiah who ministers in the heavenly Holy of holies. There, through the eyes of faith, we look upon him and ask him to intercede on our behalf—to assist us with our struggles in life, confess our sin, and receive his forgiveness. Even at times when words fail us because of the apparent complexity of a given situation, in prayer the Holy Spirit searches our hearts and carries our needs to the throne of God:

> Likewise the Spirit helps us in our weakness. For we do not know what to pray for as we ought, but the Spirit himself intercedes for us with groanings too deep for words. And he

who searches hearts knows what is the mind of the Spirit, because the Spirit intercedes for the saints according to the will of God. (Rom. 8:26–7)

Once again, even in prayer, the Word of God is instructive and helpful as an instrument in our sanctification. If words fail us and we do not know how to praise God, we can go to the Scriptures for help. Like a parent who repeats words to a child to teach her how to speak, in reading the words of Scripture back to God in prayer, we too learn how to speak to our heavenly Father.[25] While there are many different portions of the Scriptures that can assist us in our prayers, the book of Psalms is especially helpful. The Psalms were written as both songs and prayers; but like music in our own day, they capture a range of emotions and circumstances—profound joy to utter misery, from great fear to unassailable confidence.

Prayer is the crucible where we enter the heavenly Holy of holies through the mediation of Jesus Christ and bring every one of our needs, small and great, to our heavenly Father. Our heavenly Father is not one to give us stones or a serpent when we ask for bread (Matt. 7:8–11). But at the same time, we should recognize that God does not meet us in prayer to be conformed to our will. Rather, we meet God in prayer to be conformed to his will. Christ in the garden pleaded with his Father that the cup of his suffering would pass but nevertheless prayed, 'Not my will, but thine, be done' (Luke 22:42; KJV). So too we offer up our prayers and desires all the while asking our heavenly Father to conform our desires to his will. Prayer is not the realm where we try to change God's mind but where we pray that he would change ours.

But even in prayer, often presented as a solitary meeting between God and the Christian, we should realize that there is a corporate dimension. In the beginning of the Lord's Prayer, for example, Jesus teaches the church to pray, 'Our Father...' (Matt. 6:9). The opening word, the first person plural pronoun, immediately informs us that we are part of a corporate body of people who pray to the one true living God through the mediation of the one true Savior in the power of the one true Spirit. Not only do we corporately pray to God in worship, ideally, we pray for one another—we intercede on behalf of one another during times of joy, tribulation, or trial. In this respect, our individual sanctification is not a solitary event. As we pray for one another we ask our faithful Lord to sanctify us all.

Over all, the means of our sanctification is quite simple—Word, sacraments, and prayer. However, this is not to imply that all we must do is go to church, read our Bibles, and pray, and we will never struggle with sin. Our sanctification is a battle and there can and likely will be difficult periods. But in the face of difficulties we should not lose hope. Our God is greater than our sin. Moreover, some of the greatest saints in the Scriptures

How often do you pray? How often do you pray with and for others?

struggled with fear, doubt, temptation, and the like. Think, for example, about John the Baptist, who doubted that Jesus truly was the Messiah. He baptized Jesus and expected things to change dramatically. In a way, things did change, but not in a way that John had hoped. John was imprisoned, which caused him to have doubts about Jesus' identity (Matt. 11:2–6). David lamented to the Lord that he was surrounded by his enemies who persecuted and mocked him (e.g., Ps. 10). The apostle Paul cried out to the Lord in prayer asking to be delivered from his thorn in his flesh (2 Cor. 12:7–8). That we have the means of grace, therefore, does not mean that we will be free of struggle. Rather, it means that we will have the necessary spiritual sustenance to see us through our struggles.

So then, perhaps a concrete example of how all of these elements work together might be helpful. What is a parent to do if he desires to be a good father to his children and to please the Lord and be more conformed to the image of Christ in this particular aspect of his Christian walk? The father must begin with worship where he attends to the means of grace—gives diligent attention to the preaching of God's Word. Before the worship service begins, he prays that God would open his heart and ears that he would truly hear the message that will be preached. When he listens to the Word he gives careful attention to how far he falls short of God's standards when he hears the law, but he then seeks shelter from his sin and guilt in the promises of the gospel. This father also should daily feed himself the Word of God as he reads the Scriptures for his own personal benefit.

He should meditate upon the things that he reads and pray that God would give him greater understanding; he should pray that God would forgive him of his sin and fill him with a greater capacity for the fruit of the Spirit so that he would be a better father—so that he would exercise great patience, self-control, and show his family love. In the course of his Scripture reading he would likely be reminded of his need to intercede on behalf of his family, his wife and children. While a good father, for example, will discipline his children for their misbehavior, he would also pray on their behalf that God would draw them closer to Christ in their own sanctification. A father should pray that his children would heed the preaching of the Word, and in accordance with their intellectual and emotional capacities, that they would give due diligence to the daily reading of the Word and prayer. All of this activity does not guarantee a specific timetable or set of results but when done in the power of the Holy Spirit, it does provide the father with the necessary means by which he can grow in his sanctification.

For the person who struggles with lust, he must flee from anything that might cause him to stumble. This means that by all means he should avoid what the Scriptures identify as sin. Looking at pornographic images, for example, should be avoided at all costs. A man should be careful about what he places before his eyes. But at the same time, sanctification does not happen simply in fleeing from sin. From the outside, a person might be free from all external temptation but have a den of iniquity within the recesses of his mind. Therefore, not only should a person flee from sinful conduct but he should also seek Christ through the means of grace. In the face of temptation, flee to Christ—seek him in prayer and through the reading and preaching of the Scriptures.

Something that all Christians should recognize, moreover, is that regardless of the struggle, we do not struggle alone. We are part of a body, part of the church of Jesus Christ. When we find ourselves incapable of dealing with our sin on our own, then we should seek accountability and help from the pastor and elders of the congregation. We should also seek the assistance of a good Christian friend, someone we trust, someone who will earnestly pray and intercede on our behalf. As James writes, 'Therefore, confess your sins to one another and pray for one another' (James 5:16). We should never struggle alone.

CONCLUSION

If our sanctification comes through our union with Christ, then it is fed through his appointed means— Word, sacrament, and prayer. If we find ourselves struggling, could it be that we have not adequately fed

Bulimia and anorexia are not just problems with food. We can apply these categories to the Christian life. Bulimics eat food and then purge it, and anorexics simply avoid food altogether. Too many Christians will go to church, binge on Scripture, and then walk away and forget everything. Other Christians simply avoid Scripture altogether. The results of spiritual bulimia and anorexia are toxic to the Christian life.

ourselves with the true manna from heaven? Could it
be that we have not gone before the throne of God in
prayer? Could it be that we have forsaken the assembly
of the saints? Christ has prepared a grand feast before us
and it behooves us to sit, eat, and engage our Savior in
holy conversation. In so doing, as we draw nigh unto him
he will gradually transform us so that we more and more
shine forth his holiness and righteousness.

3

SANCTIFICATION UNDERMINED

In the previous two chapters we defined and applied the doctrine of sanctification. In this last and final chapter, we want to explore briefly how sanctification has been undermined. There is an old cliché, 'Often imitated, never duplicated.' This saying characterizes many of the different attempts to undermine or even replace a proper doctrine of sanctification. There are different common approaches that we find scattered throughout the history of the church, which include: self-renewal, imitation, Roman Catholicism, legalism, antinomianism, asceticism, and perfectionism. For many of these common trends, the apostle Paul's words can also describe them—namely, that they have the appearance of godliness but deny its power (2 Tim. 3:5). In other words, these different substitutes may give people the impression that a person wants to be more conformed to the image of Christ, but in reality, all such efforts are rooted, not in our union with Christ but in self.

SELF-RENEWAL

We live in an age where people believe they can do anything they set their minds to. All one has to do is walk through the isles of a book shop to peruse the hundreds of different self-help books on a host of subjects. Do you want to make more money, lose weight, improve your time management skills, acquire a new skill? All of these things are within reach. The only catch is, 'There is no free lunch.' A person has to be willing to work for what she wants to achieve. There is no simple 'get rich quick' scheme. There is no short-cut to success. If you want to shed two stone, you will have to exercise and manage your diet accordingly. Many people are able to do this and so naturally, people come to the subject of sanctification and believe that success is simply a matter of will power. A person must grab himself by his moral bootstraps, apply the right amount of pressure, and pull!

In the history of the church one of the most famous advocates of self-renewal was Charles Finney, an American itinerant revivalist of the nineteenth-century. Finney was famous for his zeal for evangelism but what many do not know are the details of his theology. Finney, for example, believed that success in evangelism was analogous to the process of growing a crop of wheat. All one has to do is apply the right methods and success is all but guaranteed.[26] What methods did Finney have in mind? For starters, preachers had to determine that they would no longer sin. Finney offered this counsel to pastors:

> I am fully convinced that until evangelists and pastors adopt, and carry out in practice, the principle of total abstinence from all sin, they will as certainly find themselves, every few months, called to do their work over again, as a temperance lecturer would who should admit the moderate use of alcohol.[27]

Finney's chief solution was that the preacher had to set a good example for his parishioners to follow. But how could people simply will themselves to stop sinning?

Finney believed that man was inherently good, albeit somewhat misguided. Moral depravity, according to Finney, was not any inherited guilt or corruption as a result of the first sin of Adam but rather selfishness and a commitment to self-gratification.[28] Finney believed, therefore, that a person's ability to believe and trust in Christ for his salvation did not require the miraculous intervention of the Holy Spirit to raise a person from spiritual death to life. Rather people have the faculties and natural abilities to offer perfect obedience to God, and all a person needs is to be persuaded to do so.[29] In regeneration, then, the Holy Spirit merely acts as an agent of persuasion—like a used car salesman trying to convince a person to purchase a car, the Holy Spirit just shows the truth, importance, and benefits of obeying God.[30] On this note, Finney writes:

> It is self-evident, that entire obedience to God's law is possible on the ground of natural ability. To deny this, is to deny that a man is able to do as well as he can. The very language of the law is such as to level its claims to the capacity of the subject, however great or small that capacity may be. 'Thou shalt love the Lord thy God with all thy heart, with all they soul, with all thy mind, and with all thy strength' (Deut. 6:5). Here then it is plain, that all the law demands is the exercise of whatever strength we have, in the service of God.[31]

Obedience to God, therefore, is simply a matter of the will. Hence, a person's sanctification is only a question of whether he wants to be more greatly conformed to the image of Christ.

According to Finney, believers have no need of union with Christ, the reading and preaching of the Word of God, or the sacraments. In Finney's understanding, such things are helpful but ultimately not determinative. Instead, a person has to desire to change and has the ability to bring about this change on his own. So many in the church would admit the need for the grace of God in sanctification, but people nevertheless try to pursue it through all too natural means. They desire to be more like

Christ and so they try harder and harder. Perhaps they employ anger management techniques, but whatever the achievement, it is ultimately fools gold—it has the appearance of gold but when finally put to the test it fails. As the old cliché goes, 'The road to hell is paved with good intentions.' Likewise, if a person does not rely upon Christ, trying harder to be holier will never produce what only Christ through the Spirit can create in us.

Have you ever approached a problem with sin apart from Christ and the gospel?

IMITATION OF CHRIST

There is another old cliché, 'Imitation is the sincerest form of flattery.' If this cliché reflects a general truth, then it is only natural that Christians would want to be more like Jesus. If Jesus sets the standard for love, then what could be better than to imitate Jesus? Should not all Christians want to be more like their Savior? A popular form of this type of approach to sanctification can be found in the recent 'What Would Jesus Do?' movement. People would wear little bracelets with the initials, 'WWJD,' inscribed upon them. When a person found himself impaled upon the horns of a moral dilemma, he would look to his bracelet to be reminded of the question, 'What would Jesus do in this situation?' The idea behind such a practice is to imitate Jesus.

But as recent as the WWJD movement is, as the Preacher tells us, there is nothing new under the sun

(Eccles. 1:9). The imitation of Christ movement as an approach to sanctification goes back at least to the Middle Ages and the famous book written by Thomas à Kempis. À Kempis believed that the way a person became more like Christ was to meditate upon his life and then try to imitate him.[32] A person was supposed to withdraw from the created world to the inner mind and contemplate Christ: 'Blessed are they who search inward things and study to prepare themselves more and more by daily exercises for receiving of heavenly mysteries.'[33] By withdrawing from the world to the inner mind, Christ would then come to a person who had prepared a mansion for him—a place to dwell. There in the inner being, Christ would hold sweet communion with the believer, impart peace, consolation, and friendship.[34]

To be sure, Christ's conduct is certainly exemplary. And properly understood, his conduct is to be imitated. But there is a world of difference in a biblical versus unbiblical imitation of Christ. À Kempis's imitation of Christ is unbiblical because he instructs people to look within—he encourages them to enter the world of mysticism. The Scriptures, on the other hand, instruct people to look without, beyond themselves to Christ. À Kempis teaches people to find their sanctification in an introspective gaze upon the self and Scripture teaches people to sanctify themselves through an extraspective gaze upon Christ. In other words, according to à Kempis, a person need not read the Scriptures or attend to the means of grace in order to seek Christ but rather only withdraw to the inner mind to find him in the subjective world of meditation. And even then, à Kempis believed that a person had to prepare a home for Christ in order to have the Savior dwell with the believer. Scripture teaches a very different picture of sanctification.

When the Holy Spirit effectually calls a person to believe in Christ, he performs the supernatural work to prepare a dwelling place for Christ. The moment a person believes he is in union with Christ. Christ has prepared his own home within the believer. Moreover, Christ does not leave the believer to fend for himself to wander in the inner recesses of the mind in order to find a consoling word from him. Christ speaks to and feeds his people through the reading and preaching of the Word and the sacraments. Like Israel of old that received water from the rock and manna from heaven to sustain them along their pilgrimage to the Promised Land, Christ sees to our every spiritual need. Through the sustenance of Word and sacrament a person is then properly equipped to imitate Christ in a biblical manner. The apostle John writes, for example: 'Beloved, do not imitate evil but imitate good. Whoever does good is from God; whoever does evil has not seen God' (3 John 11). But John is not telling his recipients merely to imitate Jesus the way a monkey imitates human actions—i.e., monkey see, monkey do. Rather, the Bible always seats our sanctification in our union with Christ. In other words, we live from life not for it. That is, we live in the knowledge and power of who we are in Christ and not in an effort to try and be who we already are.

When we come upon moral dilemmas in life and we are not sure how to proceed, we should not ask, 'What would Jesus do?' We do not have the same mission as Jesus—the Messiah and Savior of the world. We should instead ask ourselves, 'What would Jesus have me do?' Another way to state this question is, 'What does Jesus instruct his church to do in the Word of God?' If our actions violate the Word of God, then we know we should not proceed. Some matters are left to wisdom—there is not necessarily a right or wrong answer to a specific situation. When do you answer a fool according to his folly lest he become wise in his own eyes? And when do you not answer a fool according to his folly lest you become like him (Prov. 26:4–5)? Such circumstances call for prayer and wisdom. In the end, we can imitate Christ so long as we do so in a biblical manner—in reliance upon our union with Christ and the means of grace. Anything less is an unbiblical self-driven attempt to imitate Christ that will ultimately fall short.

In matters pertaining to ethics and the Christian life, we can begin with the law of God, found in Exodus 20 and Deuteronomy 5. But there are many matters in life that are not addressed by the law. For such circumstances we can appeal to the book of Proverbs, which speaks to matters of wisdom. Sometimes, we are to correct the fool, lest he be wise in his own eyes, and other times we are to remain silent, lest we become like the fool (Prov. 26:4–5). Such circumstances call for God-given wisdom.

ROMAN CATHOLICISM

'Close only counts in horse shoes and hand grenades,' is a cliché that describes the Roman Catholic understanding of sanctification. Unlike the view of Charles Finney, who believed that people did not require the grace of God to obey him, the Roman Catholic church has always affirmed the necessity of God's grace in salvation. In this basic premise Rome agrees with the Protestant Reformation. However, there is a great difference between how Rome and the Protestant Reformation believes that a person receives that grace. Historic Roman Catholic teaching believes that there are two forms of God's grace, created and uncreated. Uncreated grace is the immediate and direct power of the triune God. No person can share in the uncreated grace of God as it is the exclusive property of the trinity. Created grace, on the other hand, is the supernatural substance that the Holy Spirit creates and infuses into a person in baptism. The created grace of God is the root and source of a person's sanctification.[35] When a person receives baptism, whether he has faith in Christ or not, he receives the infused substance that begins the process of sanctification. This infused substance is also known as a habit—a disposition towards spiritual good. Beyond this basic provision, if a person needs greater spiritual strength and sustenance, he can avail himself of the Lord's Supper and the sacrament of penance. In the Lord's Supper he physically consumes the body and blood of Christ, which gives him greater spiritual strength. In the wake of sin, he can perform penance, which the Roman Catholic Church calls, 'the second plank of justification.' That is, if a person loses his justified state because of a mortal sin (such as murder or adultery), he can regain his justified status through penance.

The overall picture one finds in a Roman Catholic understanding of sanctification is that a person needs to employ the sacraments and then cooperate with God's infused grace in such a manner as to increase in holiness and righteousness until a person can make himself perfectly like Christ. As close as this sounds to the truth, it still misses it by a wide margin. The Scriptures certainly convey the importance of the use of the sacraments. But they say nothing of the infusion of a substance into us that enables us to do good. Instead, the Scriptures speak of Christ personally and really indwelling us through the work of the Holy Spirit. When we employ the sacraments, we do so understanding that they are a visible word that points us to Christ. What the word is to the ear, the sacraments are to the other senses. Moreover, the sacraments are dependent upon the preaching of the Word, the work of the Holy Spirit to apply it, and the presence of faith in the person to receive the sacrament to one's benefit. The big difference between a Roman and Protestant understanding of sanctification is the former centers upon the distribution of a substance through the sacraments and the latter centers upon the indwelling presence of Christ and his Word as it comes in its audible and visible forms. The sacraments are a vital part of growing in our sanctification, but we should properly understand how they function. They are not magical rites that change us apart from Christ and his Word—they are visible words that herald the saving work of Christ and cannot function apart from the preached Word.

One of the biggest differences between Protestants and Roman Catholics is that the latter believe that church tradition is of equal authority with Scripture. Hence, Roman Catholics can appeal to the church's authority in matters of doctrine. Protestants, however, believe that the Bible alone (sola Scriptura) is the ultimate authority in doctrine and life.

LEGALISM

Great respect for the law of God is a characteristic that should mark any Christian. At the same time, one way sanctification can be undermined is by legalism. There are a number of different kinds of legalism, but when it pertains to sanctification, the problem is seeking sanctification through the law apart from Christ. That is, there are people who believe that they will be further sanctified by their obedience to the law. In a word, they believe the law of God will sanctify them. Legalists give scrupulous attention to every minute detail of the law all in the hopes that their attentiveness will help them become more like Christ. Sanctification through the law is perhaps best exemplified in the early church's understanding of Moses's relationship to Jesus. Moses brought the law but it had strict requirements and conditions, those that no person could fulfill. Jesus, on the other hand, was viewed as a new Moses who brought a new law, one that was easier to fulfill. Only through further obedience is a person then enabled to grow in greater likeness to Christ. Proponents of legalism can hold a variety of views, but most would likely acknowledge the necessity of the grace of God.

The problem with such a view is not an appreciation of the law but rather a misunderstanding of its precise function. The law was never given as a means by which people would grow in holiness. The law was given to identify sin—the law accuses and condemns. The gospel account of Christ's encounter with lepers best illustrates the function of the law. According to the law, lepers were supposed to be cast outside the camp because they were unclean (Lev. 13). The law did nothing to change them—the law merely identified the unclean state of a leper. No matter how much a leper might pursue the law, it was powerless to heal him. There was a world of difference when the lepers looked to Christ by faith—he healed the lepers—he changed their condition. Not only did he render them clean and holy according to the law, which now permitted their presence among the people, but he also healed them of their leprosy (Luke 5:12–13; 17:12–19).

By itself, the law only identifies sin and condemns it. But when the law is preached in concert with the gospel, the two work in harmony together. The law identifies a person's sin, and through the convicting power of the Holy Spirit, a person realizes his sinfulness, and then flees to the transformative power of the gospel. And the gospel, mind you, is not simply for the entry point to the Christian life. The gospel is power unto salvation—the gospel is key not only for our initial conversion but for our entire life-long pilgrimage. Hence, for the Christian genuinely concerned for his greater conformity to Christ, the law performs a vital function. The Christian realizes that the law does not save; only Christ saves. If we understand the proper function of the law in our sanctification, then we will realize that Christ is the road on which we travel and the law is the guardrails that lets us know when we have left the roadway.

While legalism is most certainly erroneous we want to be careful that we do not become guilty of the opposite error, namely antinomianism (or lawlessness). Just because Christians are freed from the law's condemnation does not mean we have no obligation to the law. The Westminster Confession explains: 'Although true believers be not under the law, as a covenant of works, to be thereby justified, or condemned; yet it is of great use to them, as well as to others; in that, as a rule of life informing them of the will of God, and their duty, it directs and binds them to walk accordingly' (19.6).

ANTINOMIANISM

Antinomianism literally means 'against the law,' but in theological terms it denotes the belief that a Christian is no longer bound in any sense to the moral law. He is free to live as he sees fit. Moreover, a person can even engage in sinful conduct because antinomians believe that since God has justified them and forgiven their sin, they can engage in sin knowing that they are already forgiven. Perhaps one of the more famous instances of antinomianism occurs in the Scriptures. The apostle Paul sets forth the doctrine of justification and its implications in Romans 4–7. A likely question that Paul faced was, If a person has been forgiven of his sins, then why not sin all the more? Paul writes: 'What shall we say then? Are we to continue in sin that grace may abound? By no means! How can we who died to sin still live in it' (Rom. 6:1–2)? In a word, antinomianism is completely at odds with biblical teaching. Christians are not supposed to use the grace of God and the forgiveness of sins as a license for continued engagement in a sinful lifestyle.

What antinomians fail to consider is that, yes, we are forgiven of our sins in our justification—past, present, and future. Paul's words of comfort should always resound in our ears: 'There is therefore now no condemnation for those who are in Christ Jesus…Who shall bring any charge against God's elect? It is God who justifies. Who is to condemn? Christ Jesus is the one who died—more than that, who was raised—who is at the right hand of God, who indeed is interceding for us' (Rom. 8:1, 33–4). This is a glorious truth that should unshackle guilt-ridden consciences and impart great peace. However, our justification is but one part of our greater redemption, a salvation that also includes our sanctification. One of the impelling reasons behind God's redemption of his people was to vindicate his name among the nations. Israel engaged in all sorts of sinful conduct and brought shame and disrepute to the name of God. God specifically promised his people through the prophet Ezekiel: 'And I will put my Spirit within you, and cause you to walk in my statutes and be careful to obey my rules' (Ezek. 36:27).

Not only do we enjoy the forgiveness of sins but we also receive the indwelling presence of the Holy Spirit who causes us to walk in God's statutes. In simpler terms, justified Christians seek to obey God's law.

Not only do antinomians fail to understand the nature of redemption, but they also do not grasp the function of God's law, pre- and post-conversion. Before a person's conversion, the law is an enemy—it condemns sin. But once a person is saved and places his faith in Christ, the law is not completely eradicated from the life of the Christian. Rather, the condemnation of the law is completely removed. In Christ, the law becomes a friend and informs the Christian not only what God has written upon his heart, as Ezekiel prophesied, but also what conduct is pleasing to God. As much as the apostle Paul rails against legalism in Galatians, for example, he still has positive things to say about the law in the life of a Christian: 'For you were called to freedom, brothers. Only do not use your freedom as an opportunity for the flesh, but through love serve one another. For the whole law is fulfilled in one word: "You shall love your neighbor as yourself"' (Gal. 5:13–14; cf. Lev. 19:18). Likewise, James writes: 'If you really fulfill the royal law according to the Scripture, "You shall love your neighbor as yourself," you are doing well' (James 2:8; cf. Lev. 19:18). James and Paul echo the words of Christ when he was asked what the greatest commandment was: 'You shall love the Lord your God with all your heart and with all your soul and with all your mind. This is the great and first commandment. And a second is like it: You shall love your neighbor as yourself. On these two commandments depend all the Law and the Prophets' (Matt. 22:37–40; cf. Deut. 6:4; Lev. 19:18).

In technical terms, theologians have labeled the three different functions of the law in the following manner. The political use of the law is the knowledge man has of God's law through nature as it is inscribed upon his heart (Rom. 2:13–14). The political use of the law governs societies. No matter how pagan a people might be, they know that stealing is wrong. Even thieves who might try to deny that thievery is wrong will bitterly complain when someone steals from them. The pedagogical use of the law serves to identify and condemn sin with the goal of driving the sinner to Christ. In this use of the law, the law and gospel work in tandem, as the law condemns and the gospel forgives sin. The normative use, also commonly called the third use, of the law shows the redeemed sinner what conduct is good, acceptable, and pleasing to God. The Christian can employ the law only in this manner because Christ has met the demands of the law both in his fulfillment of it as well as in paying the penalty for its violation.

ASCETICISM

Asceticism is the practice of denying one's self material and physical pleasures, even those that are not evil or sinful. The basic belief is that in order to grow in sanctification a person has to deny himself various creature comforts that might soften one's resolve in the battle against sin. Hence, a person might move to the rural countryside because he perceives the city to be filled with sin. Or because of the corruption of sexuality, a person might avoid marriage altogether because he would not want to engage in sexual intercourse because of its perceived connections to evil. People will refrain from the consumption of alcohol because of its perceived identification with evil. In a word, asceticism might be described as sanctification by the flight from perceived evils. To be sure, all Christians should flee from sinful conduct. Christians often engage in gross sin because they dally in borderline conduct. They initially excuse small sins, such as so-called 'white lies,' but then quickly find themselves comfortable with big lies. However, it is an entirely different proposition to believe that one's sanctification consists merely in the flight from sin.

Sanctification is grounded in our union with the risen and ascended Christ. True, we should flee from sin, but we must also draw near to Christ through his appointed means—Word, sacrament, and prayer (Acts 2:42, 46–7; Ps. 19:8; 2 Cor. 10:4–6; Eph. 6:16–17). Additionally, Christians must learn to distinguish between sin and good, unrighteousness and righteousness. Take sexuality, for example. Within the bonds of marriage, sexuality is a good and holy thing, designed by God as an expression of love between husband and wife and for the propagation of the human race. There is an entire book of the Bible devoted to exploring sexuality within marriage,

Song of Solomon. A person can look around him and determine that his city is filled with corruption and sin. If he desires to move away, he must recognize that he might mitigate the amount of sin he sees on a daily basis, but in the end, he will always carry his problem with sin with him. Every time we look into the mirror, we behold the face of our worst enemy. Until the completion of our sanctification we will constantly struggle with sin because the remnants of our defeated sinful nature remain within us. You can take the man out of the sinful city, but you cannot take the sin out of the man simply with a change of geography. Christ addressed this type of issue when he said: 'What comes out of a person is what defiles him. For from within, out of the heart of man, come evil thoughts, sexual immorality, theft, murder, adultery, coveting, wickedness, deceit, sensuality, envy, slander, pride, foolishness. All these evil things come from within, and they defile a person' (Mark 7:20–23).

Only Christ, through the application of the Holy Spirit, cleanses a man from sin. Hence, a person can freely eat and consume whatever he pleases, even such things as alcohol. The Scriptures condemn the abuse of alcohol, drunkenness, not the responsible enjoyment of it (Rom. 13:13; Gal. 5:21; 1 Pet. 4:3). A person might decide to refrain from the consumption of alcohol, not because he believes it will make him holier, but out of concern for a weaker brother or sister in Christ (Rom 14:13–23). In other words, if a new Christian is a recovering alcoholic, then it might be entirely appropriate and loving to refrain from drinking alcohol in this person's presence so as not to create a stumbling block to him by creating a scenario where he might be tempted to abuse alcohol.

Paul's counsel against asceticism is noteworthy:

> If with Christ you died to the elemental spirits of the world, why, as if you were still alive in the world, do you submit to regulations—'Do not handle, Do not taste, Do not touch' (referring to things that all perish as they are used)—according to human precepts and teachings? These have indeed an appearance of wisdom in promoting self-made religion and asceticism and severity to the body, but they are of no value in stopping the indulgence of the flesh. (Col. 2:20–23)

In many ways, asceticism is a cousin to legalism. Ascetics refrain from enjoying things that God has intended to be used, consumed, and enjoyed. Rather than going beyond what God has commanded, in our pursuit of greater sanctification we should avoid what the Scriptures have clearly identified as sin and flee to Christ, the only one who can transform us into his glorious image.

Have you ever stopped to ask why God gave you your senses, taste and sight? He could have just as easily made food tasteless and odorless, and the world black and white. One of the reasons God gave us senses is to explore the beauty, splendor, tastes, and fragrances of the good creation.

PERFECTIONISM

The last of the efforts to undermine the doctrine of sanctification is perfectionism, which is the teaching that a person can become sin-free before his glorification. In other words, some Christians have the ability to mature eventually to the point where they refrain from sin. This teaching most famously originated with the eighteenth-century pastor-evangelist, John Wesley.[36] I remember one of my seminary professors telling a story of a student who informed him that he had ceased from sinning. My professor bluntly confronted the student with the statement, 'Well, that's too bad for you, because you just sinned in making that admission.' In other words, as long as we live in this world, this side of glory, we will always be engaged in a battle against sin. The apostle John states this truth rather forcefully when he writes: 'If we say we have no sin, we deceive ourselves, and the truth is not in us' (1 John 1:8). Why do we continually fight against sin in the battle for our sanctification?

The short answer is that we have not been glorified. Or in Pauline terms, we have been raised according to our 'inner man,' but as Paul explains, our outer man is still wasting away (2 Cor. 4:16). In other words, we still carry about this body of death, and it is not until we are glorified and receive our renewed outer man that we will be completely freed of all sin. This means that there is never a single fraction of a second in our lives when we are not utterly and totally dependent upon our union with Christ for our continued growth in sanctification.

We will always struggle with sin. Though, this is not to say that we will struggle with the same sins. God willing, as we mature, the sins we battle in our early Christian life are not the same sins we struggle with in our later walk with Christ. A new Christian might struggle with controlling his tongue whereas a mature Christian likely will not. At the root of perfectionism lies the dangerous sin of pride, as the one who claims perfection will likely believe he is superior to other Christians. But if we all recognize that no one can reach perfection apart from our Spirit-wrought glorification then we will likely be humbler in the admission that we always need Christ.

CONCLUSION

Despite all of the efforts throughout the ages to find substitutes for the doctrine of sanctification, there is nothing that can replace the vital union that believers share with Christ. No amount of human effort can transform a sinner. Sanctification is not merely a question of will power. Sanctification is not merely the imitation of Christ. Even though Christ is a moral-ethical example for all Christians to follow, there is a right and wrong way to follow his example. Only when we rely upon Christ's sanctifying power by faith, fed by word, sacrament, and prayer, do we find Christ producing holiness and righteousness within us. And even then, the sacraments function only in conjunction with the word through faith—they are not magical potions to be consumed but signs and seals of God's covenantal redemption in

Christ. The law is no substitute for the Holy Spirit—the law by itself has no power to save but only condemn. Only when the Spirit applies the law with the gospel can the law be of benefit for our sanctification. The law apart from Christ is an enemy; only in Christ, who has met its demands, is it a friend. Anyone who has been redeemed by Christ, therefore, would never use the gospel as a cover-up for sin or lawlessness. On the other hand, neither is sanctification merely a flight from sin. Rather our sanctification is a continuous, relentless flight to Christ, the only one who has the power to transform and conform us to his holy image, a transformation that only occurs on the final day, and never before. In a word, accept no substitutes for a Spirit-wrought sanctification rooted in union with Christ and fed by the means of grace.

SUGGESTIONS FOR FURTHER READING

The Preacher was certainly correct when he once wrote: 'Of making many books there is no end, and much study is a weariness of the flesh' (Eccles. 12:12). There is an ocean of theological literature, more than any one person can possibly read in a lifetime. However, from this vast ocean we can scoop a thimble-full of books that can help Christians learn more about the doctrine of sanctification.

ENTRY-LEVEL

John Murray, *Redemption Accomplished and Applied*. Grand Rapids: Eerdmans, 1955.

Murray's little book is a wonderful survey of the work of Christ and how it is applied in our redemption in the order of salvation. Each of the chapters are brief and non-technical. This book could easily be used for personal study, small groups, or for a basic introduction to the doctrine of salvation, of which sanctification is but one part.

Geerhardus Vos, *Grace and Glory: Sermons Preached in the Chapel of Princeton Theological Seminary.* Edinburgh: Banner of Truth, 1994.

There is no substitute for participation in worship on each and every Lord's Day and hearing the preached word. However, a terrific supplement comes in the form of written sermons. Vos offers Christ-centered sermons that provide us with manna from heaven, which is vital for our sanctification. My advice would be to skip the first sermon, as it is somewhat difficult to follow; read it last. The others are clear and a well-spring of gospel-preaching.

Vos was on faculty at Princeton with B. B. Warfield, the 'great lion of Princeton,' and also taught Louis Berkhof. Berkhof told others that Vos was one of his favorite professors and one that was formative upon his theological development.

ADVANCED

Louis Berkhof, *Systematic Theology: New Combined Edition.* Grand Rapids: Eerdmans, 1996.

For almost seventy years, Berkhof's *Systematic Theology* has been a standard theological textbook in Reformed and

Evangelical Seminaries. Several generations of ministers and theological students have cut their theological teeth on Berkhof. If you want to learn solid Reformed theology, that is, doctrine that is driven by scriptural exegesis, then Berkhof is certainly the place to go. His writing style is terse, but in academic theology, this is a virtue. Chapters are relatively brief so you can cover a specific subject in a relatively short number of pages. If you can, obtain the volume listed here as it is a combined edition, one that includes Berkhof's introductory volume to Systematic Theology, which was originally a separate volume and covers first principles (i.e., prolegomena) and the doctrine of Scripture.

Michael Horton, *The Christian Faith: A Systematic Theology for Pilgrims on the Way*. Grand Rapids: Zondervan, 2011.

What some might not know is that very few Reformed systematic theologies have been written in the last seventy years since Berkhof released his volume in the late 1930's. Horton's volume, therefore, is a noteworthy contribution as it goes into greater exegetical depth, offers helpful insights about theology, and engages with conservative and liberal contemporary theology. But Horton also locates the various doctrines in Scripture within the broader story of the unfolding plan of redemption. Horton's work is not for the faint of heart, as it weighs in at over 1,000 pages. But it is clearly written and a helpful glossary in the back of the book offers the neophyte a handy resource in his quest to learn theology.

CLASSIC WORKS

Walter Marshall, *The Gospel Mystery of Sanctification*. Grand Rapids: Reformation Heritage Books, 1999.

Walter Marshall, *The Gospel Mystery of Sanctification: A New Version, Put Into Modern English* by Bruce H. McRae. Eugene: Wipf & Stock, 2005.

John Murray reportedly said that this book was the most important book on sanctification that had ever been written. While I cannot confirm this opinion, as I have only dipped my toes in the ocean of theological literature, I can certainly say that it is one of the best that I have ever read. Marshall wrote his work in the midst of the neonomian and antinomian controversies of the seventeenth century. He rode the razor's edge and avoided legalism on the one hand and lawlessness on the other. He firmly roots the believer's sanctification in the life-giving union with Christ but also discusses the all-important relationship between justification and sanctification. There are two versions of this book, the 1999 Reformation Heritage version, which is a reproduction of the original text in a contemporary font; the second is a modern English edition. The former, if you are not used to it, can be a slow read; the latter is very readable.

Edward Fisher, *The Marrow of Modern Divinity*. Fearn: Christian Focus, 2009.

A cliché I have found to be true is that great books are often out of print, but in this case the sentiment is happily disproven. Originally published in 1645 during controversies in London regarding antinomianism and legalism, Fisher set forth to cut a middle path between the two erroneous extremes by writing a dialog between an antinomian, Antinomista, a legalist, Nomista, and a proponent of the true gospel, Evangelista. What makes this dialogue so helpful is that Fisher often engages common questions, criticisms, and related issues that pertain to the gospel, justification, sanctification, and the believer's relationship to the law of God. Part II of the work contains an exposition of the Ten Commandments. Additionally, he also situates the doctrine of salvation within the unfolding plan of redemption, by relating it to the covenants of works and grace. What makes this particular edition of the *Marrow of Modern Divinity* noteworthy is it is in a handsome hardbound edition, cleanly typeset, and has an excellent preface and introduction that explains the importance and significance of the work.

CONCLUSION

There are certainly many other noteworthy books that deal with sanctification, either directly or indirectly. However, the above-mentioned books are certainly excellent places to start. One might begin with Murray's *Redemption Accomplished and Applied*, and follow with Marshall and Fisher, though these books should supplement and never replace the daily reading of Scripture. Contemporary books are certainly helpful, but I am particularly fond of old books, as they often address and emphasize truths our own age has forgotten. And reading old books helps us to take advantage of our rich theological tradition. As G. K. Chesterton once wrote: 'Tradition means giving votes to the most obscure of all classes, our ancestors. It is the democracy of the dead. Tradition refuses to submit to the small and arrogant oligarchy of those who happen to be walking about.'[37] So, then, *tolle et lege*, take up and read! Stand on the shoulders of giants! Sit at the feet of some of the greatest theological minds by which God has blessed the church and learn more about your sanctification.

ENDNOTES

1 Quotations of the Westminster Standards are taken from *The Confession of Faith and Catechisms: The Westminster Confession of Faith and Catechisms as adopted by The Orthodox Presbyterian Church with Proof Texts* (Willow Grove: The Committee on Christian Education of the OPC, 2005).

2 Louis Berkhof, *Systematic Theology: Combined Edition* (1932–38; Grand Rapids: Eerdmans, 1996), 449.

3 The Catechism cites Rom. 8:30, Eph. 1:5, 1 Cor. 1:30, 6:11.

4 John Murray, *Redemption Accomplished and Applied* (Grand Rapids: Eerdmans, 1955), 79–80.

5 The Catechism cites Rom. 3:24, 4:6–8; 2 Cor. 5:19, 21; Rom. 4:6, 11, 5:19; Gal. 2:16; Phil. 3:9

6 Berkhof, *Systematic Theology*, 513–14.

7 Heidelberg Catechism, in *Ecumenical and Reformed Creeds and Confessions: Classroom Edition* (Dyer: Mid-America Reformed Seminary, 1991).

8 Wilhelmus à Brakel, *The Christian's Reasonable Service*, 4 vols., trans. Bartel Elshout (Pittsburgh: Soli Deo Gloria, 1994), 3.4.

9   Calvin, *Institutes of the Christian Religion*, LCC, vols. 20–21, trans. Ford Lewis Battles, ed. John T. McNeill (Philadelphia: Westminster, 1960), 3.11.1.

10   John Calvin, *Institutes of the Christian Religion*, 3 vols., trans. John Allen (Philadelphia: Philip H. Hicklin, 1816), 3.17.9.

11   Murray, *Redemption Accomplished*, 87.

12   Calvin, *Institutes* (Battles), 3.11.1.

13   See J. Todd Billings, *Calvin, Participation, and the Gift: The Activity of Believers in Union with Christ* (Oxford: OUP, 2007), 106–7.

14   Charles Hodge, *Systematic Theology*, 3 vols. (rep.; Grand Rapids: Eerdmans, 1991), 3.218.

15   The Confession cites John 1:12; Acts 16:31; Gal. 2:20; Acts 15:11; 2 Tim. 1:9–10.

16   Murray, *Redemption Accomplished*, 147.

17   Walter Marshall, *The Gospel Mystery of Sanctification* (1692; Grand Rapids: Reformation Heritage Books, 1999), 69.

18   Marshall (ed. McRae), *Gospel Mystery*, 187; cf. idem, *Gospel Mystery*, 181.

19   John Owen, *On the Mortification of Sin in Believers*, in *The Works of John Owen*, vol. 7 (London: Richard Baynes, 1826), 335–6.

20   Owen, *Mortification of Sin*, 377–84.

21   Owen, *Mortification of Sin*, 384.

22   Owen, *Mortification of Sin*, 420.

23   See G. K. Beale, *We Become What We Worship: A Biblical Theology of Idolatry* (Downers Grove: IVP Academic, 2008), 15–140.

24   The Catechism cites Neh. 8:8; Acts 28:18; Ps. 19:8; 1 Cor. 14:24–5; 2 Chron. 34:18–19, 26–8; Acts 2:37, 41, 8:27–38; 2 Cor. 3:18; Col. 1:27; 2 Cor. 10:4–6; Rom. 6:17–18; Eph. 6:16–17; Col. 1:28; Ps. 19:11; Matt. 4:4, 7, 10; 1 Cor. 10:11; Eph. 4:11–12; Acts 20:32; 2 Tim. 3:15–17; Rom. 16:25; 1 Thess. 3:2, 10–11, 13.

25   Dietrich Bonhoeffer, *Prayerbook of the Bible*, in *Dietrich Bonhoeffer Works*, vol. 5, trans. James H. Burtness, ed. Geffrey B. Kelly (Minneapolis: Fortress, 1996), 155–6.

26   Charles G. Finney, *Lectures on Revivals of Religion*, ed. William G. McLoughlin (1835; Cambridge: Harvard University Press, 1960), 33.

27   Charles G. Finney, *Finney's Systematic Theology: The Complete and Newly Expanded 1878 Edition*, eds. Dennis Carroll, Bill Nicely, and L. G. Parkhurst (1878; Minneapolis: Bethany House, 1994), 395.

28   Finney, *Systematic Theology*, 245, 327.

29   Finney, *Systematic Theology*, 271-72.

30   Finney, *Systematic Theology*, 276.

31   Finney, *Systematic Theology*, 382.

32   Thomas à Kempis, *The Imitation of Christ* (n. c.: Filiquarian Publishing, 2005), 1.1.1.

33   À Kempis, *Imitation of Christ*, 2.1.1.

34   À Kempis, *Imitation of Christ*, 2.1.1.

35   Joseph Cardinal Ratzinger, ed., *Catechism of the Catholic Church* (Ligouri: Liberria Editrice Vaticana, 1992), § 1999, p. 484.

36   See John Wesley, *A Plain Account of Christian Perfection* (New York: G. Lane and P. P. Sandford, 1844).

37   G. K. Chesterton, *Orthodoxy: The Romance of Faith* (1959; New York: Doubleday, 1990), 48.

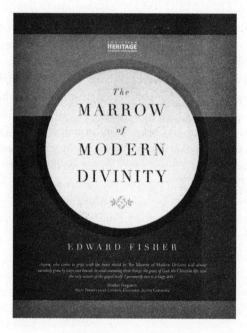

The
MARROW
of
MODERN
DIVINITY

EDWARD FISHER

*Anyone, who comes to grips with the issues raised in The Marrow of Modern Divinity will almost
inevitably grow by leaps and bounds. In understanding these things, the grace of God, the Christian life, and
the very nature of the gospel itself. I personally owe it a huge debt.*

Sinclair Ferguson
First Presbyterian Church, Columbia, North Carolina

ISBN 978-1-84550-479-3

The Marrow of Modern Divinity

Edward Fisher

An intriguing book, quite unlike any other *The Marrow of Modern Divinity* defies pigeonholing. It was written in the 1600s by an author of whom we know little, yet it proved to be a critically important and controversial theological text.

Penned as dialogue between a minister(Evangelista), a young Christian(Neophytus), a legalist(Nomista) who believes Christianity is a set of rules to be obeyed and Antinomista who thinks it's okay to sin because God will forgive him anyway, it makes for a wonderfully insightful book that remains tremendously relevant for our world today.

This newly laid out and eagerly awaited edition includes explanatory notes by the famous puritan Thomas Boston, an Introduction by Philip Ryken and an historical Introduction by William Vandoodewaard.

Anyone who comes to grips with the issues raised in *The Marrow of Modern Divinity* will almost certainly grow by leaps and bounds in understanding three things: the grace of God, the Christian life, and the very nature of the gospel itself. I personally owe it a huge debt. Despite their mild-mannered appearance, these pages contain a powerful piece of propaganda. Read them with great care!

Sinclair B. Ferguson,
Senior Minister, First Presbyterian Church,
Columbia, South Carolina

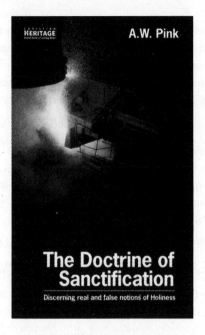

A.W. Pink

The Doctrine of Sanctification

Discerning real and false notions of Holiness

ISBN 978-1-85792-414-5

The Doctrine of Sanctification

Discerning real and false notions of Holiness

A. W. PINK

A.W. Pink is acknowledged as one of the deeper think-ers of his era on subjects of doctrine and Christian living. He felt only able to write this book after studying the subject for over 25 years; previous to this he felt he was too immature and unscriptural.

Questions answered in this book include – Is sanctification something believers have, or something they experience?

How is it obtained – is it done for us, by us, or both? How may you be assured that you have been sanctified? Is there any difference between sanctification by the Fa-ther, Son, Spirit, faith and the Word?

Is there any difference between sanctification and holiness?

Does sanctification relate to the soul, or the body, or both?

What is the connection between regeneration and sanc-tification?

What is the relationship between justification and sanc-tification?

Does sanctification precede or follow salvation, or is it an integral part of it?

Why are the above important and why do so many peo-ple disagree on the subject?

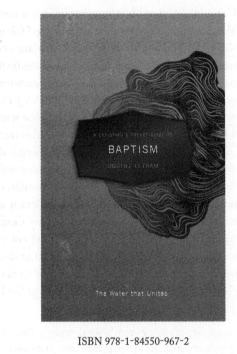

A CHRISTIAN'S POCKET GUIDE TO

BAPTISM

ROBERT LETHAM

The Water that Unites

ISBN 978-1-84550-967-2

A Christian's Pocket Guide to Baptism

ROBERT LETHAM

What is Christian baptism? Is it, as many believe, a mere symbol? When should someone be baptized? In *A Christian's Pocket Guide to Baptism*, Robert Letham answers such questions from Scripture. He reflects sensitively on historic Christian teaching and avoids the extremes that often mark discussions of this subject, making this a book for everyone. Letham's plain talk will not leave beginners bemused, nor will it frustrate those who want to make real progress in their theological understanding. It is a 'tragedy', says Letham, that Christians should think of baptism as 'the water that divides'. The sign of our union with Christ should unite Christians, not least because it does not focus on our actions, but on God's mighty deeds. Baptism belongs to him. It must always be administered in connection with faith, yet that does not mean Christians do anything to receive or to earn baptism. They are to be baptized solely because of God's gracious promises.

Here is a robust, articulate and biblical presentation of covenant baptism that avoids populism and individualism. Dr Letham has placed baptism in its covenantal and canonical context - a work of God rather than an act of obedience - no bare sign but an active means of grace - for believers and their children.

Liam Goligher, Senior Minister,
Tenth Presbyterian Church, Philadelphia, Pennsylvania

A CHRISTIAN'S POCKET GUIDE TO

JESUS CHRIST

MARK JONES

An Introduction to Christology

ISBN 978-1-84550-951-4

A Christian's Pocket Guide to Jesus Christ

Mark Jones

For many of us, the whole concept of Christology is as mystifying as a foreign language, yet Christians down the ages have fought to defend the person and work of Christ - seeing him and what he did quite rightly as a vital element of how we are saved. If we are to understand this subject we need to know the person of Christ; not just what he did (his work) but who he is (his person). Through this book we get to know the Son of God who indeed is God and not just a superman! He is the one who came from above and became fully human having a human body and soul. Being God enabled him to pay the debt owed for sin and being man enabled him to stand on man's behalf for their sin. In straightforward and simple layman terms this book will explain the interconnectivity of the work and person of Jesus Christ and dispel any misconceptions you may have

Who is Jesus Christ? Our answer to that question will determine our eternity. What we believe about Jesus is essential to our belief in Jesus. In this book, Dr. Mark Jones helps to answer hard questions about the person and work of Jesus Christ in a simple and clear manner. This book is an excellent tool for evangelism and discipleship, and it is a much-needed resource for new believers, laypeople, and pastors alike.

Burk Parsons, Associate Pastor,
Saint Andrews Chapel, Sanford, Florida

Christian Focus Publications

publishes books for all ages. Our mission statement –

STAYING FAITHFUL

In dependence upon God we seek to impact the world through literature faithful to His infallible Word, the Bible. Our aim is to ensure that the Lord Jesus Christ is presented as the only hope to obtain forgiveness of sin, live a useful life and look forward to heaven with Him.

REACHING OUT

Christ's last command requires us to reach out to our world with His gospel. We seek to help fulfil that by publishing books that point people towards Jesus and help them develop a Christ-like maturity. We aim to equip all levels of readers for life, work, ministry and mission.

Books in our adult range are published in three imprints:

Christian Focus contains popular works including biographies, commentaries, basic doctrine and Christian living. Our children's books are also published in this imprint.

Mentor focuses on books written at a level suitable for Bible College and seminary students, pastors, and other serious readers. The imprint includes commentaries, doctrinal studies, examination of current issues and church history.

Christian Heritage contains classic writings from the past.

Christian Focus Publications Ltd,
Geanies House, Fearn, Ross-shire,
IV20 1TW, Scotland, United Kingdom.
www.christianfocus.com